artworld

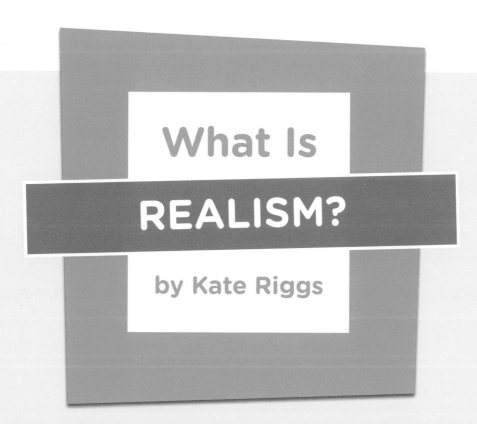

What Is REALISM?

by Kate Riggs

CREATIVE EDUCATION • CREATIVE PAPERBACKS

Published by Creative Education and Creative Paperbacks
P.O. Box 227, Mankato, Minnesota 56002
Creative Education and Creative Paperbacks are
imprints of The Creative Company
www.thecreativecompany.us

Design and production by Chelsey Luther
Art direction by Rita Marshall
Printed in the United States of America

Photographs by Alamy (Visual Arts Library [London]), Art Resource
(The Metropolitan Museum of Art/Art Resource, NY), The Athenaeum
(Henry Ossawa Tanner), The Bridgeman Art Library (Christie's Images/
Bridgeman Images), Corbis (Jules Adolphe Aime Louis Breton/Brooklyn
Museum), Getty Images (Apic, Gustave Courbet, Jean-Francois Millet),
Wikimedia Creative Commons (Jean-Baptiste Camille Corot/National
Gallery of Art/Scewing, Gustave Courbet/The Yorck Project: 10.000
Meisterwerke der Malerei/Aavindraa)

Library of Congress Cataloging-in-Publication Data
Riggs, Kate.
What is realism? / Kate Riggs.
p. cm. — (Art world)
Summary: With prompting questions and historical background, an
early reader comes face to face with famous works of Realist art and is
encouraged to identify actions and consider everyday events.
Includes bibliographical references and index.
ISBN 978-1-60818-628-0 (hardcover)
ISBN 978-1-62832-226-2 (pbk)
ISBN 978-1-56660-694-3 (eBook)
1. Realism in art—Juvenile literature. 2. Painting, Modern—19th century—
Juvenile literature. I. Title.

ND192.R4R54 2016
751.4—dc23   2015008503

CCSS: RI.1.1, 2, 3, 5, 6, 7; RI.2.1, 2, 3, 5, 6, 7; RI.3.1, 3, 5, 7; RF.1.1; RF.2.3, 4;
RF.3.3

First Edition HC
9 8 7 6 5 4 3 2 1
First Edition PBK
9 8 7 6 5 4 3 2 1

Contents

Children play.

People and Places

People gather crops. Can you almost hear the noise? If you see people doing real-life things, you may be looking at a Realist painting.

Sledging on a Frozen Pond (c. 1900), by Peder Monsted

Art in Life

The Realists painted life as they saw it. They wanted to show how everyday people lived. Most of the art before Realism was about emotions or history. The Realists just wanted the facts.

The End of the Working Day (1886–87), by Jules Breton

The Sleeping Embroiderer (1853), by Courbet

Realist Reactions

Realism started in France. Gustave Courbet and his friends did not want to paint made-up stories. They wanted to show people at work, sleep, or play.

Courbet's original *Stone Breakers* was destroyed in World War II.

Picking Apart

One day, Courbet saw two men breaking apart stone. He painted *The Stone Breakers* (1849). The canvas was more than five feet (1.5 m) tall! It was like looking at life-sized people.

Look at the Face

A German named Wilhelm Leibl painted lifelike scenes, too. He drew *Three Women in Church* (1878–82). Look at each woman's face. Each has a different expression. They do not wear fancy clothes.

Leibl watched people as they prayed and read.

The boys are playing snap the whip at recess.

Playtime

Have you ever played a game called snap the whip? American Winslow Homer showed boys playing that in 1872. Some of the boys hang on. But one has just fallen down!

Simple Subjects

Poor people did not often get their pictures painted. Henry Ossawa Tanner's *The Thankful Poor* (1894) helped change that. A man and a boy sit down to a simple meal. Tanner shows light shining over them.

Tanner shows that these people are thankful for what they have.

Young Girl Reading (c. 1868), by Camille Corot

Realism and You

What do you see around you? Think about the places you go every day. Could your life be a Realist painting?

Portrait of a Realist

Robert Henri was born in Ohio in 1865. He became an art teacher. Henri thought American painters should show what life was like in the cities. He painted snowy streets. He painted people in everyday and fancy clothes.

Left: *Skipper Mick* (1924); above: *Gertrude Vanderbilt Whitney* (1916)

Glossary

canvas—a piece of strong cloth on which people can paint

emotions—feelings such as happiness, sadness, fearfulness, and excitement

expression—the look on someone's face; expressions may be happy, sad, or another emotion

Read More

Kohl, MaryAnn F., and Kim Solga. *Discovering Great Artists: Hands-on Art for Children in the Styles of the Great Masters*. Bellingham, Wash.: Bright Ring, 1996.

Venezia, Mike. *Winslow Homer*. New York: Children's Press, 2004.

Websites

NGAkids Art Zone
http://www.nga.gov/content/ngaweb/education/kids.html
Make your own art, and learn more about Realism at the National Gallery of Art.

Sing-along at the Metropolitan Museum of Art
http://www.metmuseum.org/metmedia/kids-zone/start-with -art/sing-along
Sing along to identify paintings by famous artists.

NOTE: Every effort has been made to ensure that the websites listed above are suitable for children, that they have educational value, and that they contain no inappropriate material. However, because of the nature of the Internet, it is impossible to guarantee that these sites will remain active indefinitely or that their contents will not be altered.

Index